Table of Contents

Chapter 1: The Need for Educational Reform 4

Chapter 2: Understanding Artificial Intelligence in Education 12

Chapter 3: The Role of Teachers in an AI-Driven Classroom 20

Chapter 4: Designing the AI Learning Environment . 28

Chapter 5: Curriculum Development for Lifelong Learning 36

Chapter 6: Student-Centered Learning Approaches ... 44

Chapter 7: Assessment and Evaluation in an AI Framework 52

Chapter 8: Year-Round Learning Models 59

Chapter 9: Community Involvement and Support Systems 66

Chapter 10: Addressing Equity and Accessibility Issues 74

Chapter 11: Global Perspectives on AI in Education . 82

Chapter 12: Future Trends in Educational Technology 89

Chapter 13: Psychological Aspects of AI-Assisted Learning..97

Chapter 14: Policy Implications for Educational Reform..105

Chapter 15: Case Studies of Successful Implementations 113

Chapter 16: Challenges to Implementation 120

Chapter 17: The Role of Research in Evolving Education...128

Chapter 18: Envisioning the Future of Education 136

Sinopse 146

2.

3.

4.

5.

6.

7.

8.

9.

10.

11.

12.

13.

14.

15.

16.

17.

18.

19.

20.

1

The Need for Educational Reform

1.1 Historical Context of Education

The historical context of education is crucial for understanding the need for reform in contemporary educational systems. Over centuries, education has evolved from informal, community-based learning to structured systems governed by state policies and societal needs. This evolution reflects broader social, economic, and technological changes that have shaped how knowledge is imparted and acquired.

In ancient civilizations, such as those in Mesopotamia and Egypt, education was primarily reserved for the elite. Knowledge was transmitted orally or through written texts on clay tablets or papyrus. The focus was often on practical skills necessary for governance or trade rather than a holistic approach to learning. As societies progressed into the Middle Ages, the establishment of universities marked a significant shift towards formalized education, emphasizing theology, philosophy, and later sciences.

Â The Industrial Revolution brought about another transformation in education. With the rise of factories and urbanization, there was an increasing demand for a literate workforce capable of performing specialized tasks. This led to the introduction of compulsory schooling laws in many countries during the 19th century. Education became more standardized with age-based grade levels and a curriculum focused on reading, writing, arithmetic, and vocational training.

Â However, despite these advancements, traditional educational models have often been criticized for their rigidity and inability to adapt to individual learning styles or the rapidly changing demands of society. The late 20th century saw movements advocating for progressive education that emphasized critical thinking over rote memorization. Yet even these reforms struggled against entrenched systems resistant to change.

Today's educational landscape is at a crossroads where technology plays an increasingly pivotal role in shaping learning experiences. The integration of artificial intelligence into education presents an opportunity to break free from outdated paradigms by personalizing learning pathways and fostering independent knowledge acquisition among students. Understanding this historical context not only highlights past challenges but also underscores the urgency for innovative solutions that align with contemporary needs.

1.2 Limitations of the Current System

 The current educational system, while having evolved significantly over time, is fraught with limitations that hinder its effectiveness in meeting the diverse needs of students. These constraints not only affect individual learners but also have broader implications for society as a whole. Understanding these limitations is crucial for advocating meaningful reform.

 One of the most pressing issues is the rigidity of standardized curricula, which often fails to accommodate different learning styles and paces.

Students are frequently subjected to a one-size-fits-all approach that prioritizes uniformity over personalization. This can lead to disengagement among students who may excel in non-traditional subjects or require alternative methods of instruction. For instance, creative thinkers and kinesthetic learners often find themselves stifled by conventional teaching methods that emphasize rote memorization and standardized testing.

Â Moreover, the emphasis on high-stakes testing has created an environment where teaching to the test becomes commonplace. Educators may feel pressured to focus on test preparation rather than fostering critical thinking and problem-solving skills essential for real-world applications. This narrow focus can diminish the quality of education, as it sidelines important subjects such as arts and physical education, which contribute to a well-rounded educational experience.

Â Another significant limitation lies in resource disparities across different regions and demographics. Schools in affluent areas often benefit from better funding, advanced technology, and experienced educators compared to those in underprivileged communities. This inequity perpetuates cycles of disadvantage and limits opportunities for many students who could otherwise thrive given adequate support.

Additionally, there is a growing disconnect between educational outcomes and workforce demands. Many graduates enter the job market ill-prepared for contemporary challenges due to outdated curricula that do not reflect current technological advancements or industry needs. As automation and artificial intelligence reshape various sectors, educational institutions must adapt swiftly; however, many remain entrenched in traditional models that resist change.

In summary, addressing these limitations requires a comprehensive reevaluation of educational practices and policies aimed at creating more inclusive, adaptive systems that prepare students not just academically but holistically for their futures.

1.3 Vision for a New Learning Paradigm

The vision for a new learning paradigm is rooted in the recognition that education must evolve to meet the complexities of modern society. This paradigm shift emphasizes personalized, experiential, and collaborative learning experiences that cater to the diverse needs of students. By moving away from traditional models, we can create an educational landscape that fosters creativity, critical thinking, and adaptability—skills essential for success in an ever-changing world.

 At the core of this new paradigm is the concept of learner-centered education. This approach prioritizes individual student interests and strengths, allowing them to take ownership of their learning journey. For instance, project-based learning enables students to engage deeply with subjects by working on real-world problems that resonate with their lives. Such methods not only enhance engagement but also cultivate essential skills like teamwork and problem-solving.

 Moreover, technology plays a pivotal role in this vision. The integration of digital tools can facilitate personalized learning pathways tailored to each student's pace and style. Adaptive learning technologies can assess student progress in real-time, providing immediate feedback and resources suited to their unique needs. This dynamic interaction between learners and technology creates opportunities for deeper understanding and mastery of content.

Collaboration among educators is equally vital in this new framework. Professional development should focus on equipping teachers with innovative pedagogical strategies that promote interdisciplinary teaching and holistic education. Schools could adopt community-based approaches where educators collaborate with local organizations to enrich curricula with practical experiences that connect classroom knowledge to societal issues.

Finally, assessment practices must transform alongside instructional methods. Moving beyond standardized testing towards formative assessments allows educators to gauge student understanding continuously while providing constructive feedback aimed at growth rather than mere performance metrics. This shift encourages a culture of lifelong learning where mistakes are viewed as opportunities for improvement rather than failures.

In summary, envisioning a new learning paradigm involves reimagining educational practices that prioritize personalization, collaboration, and innovation—ultimately preparing students not just academically but as engaged citizens ready to navigate the complexities of contemporary life.

2

Understanding Artificial Intelligence in Education

2.1 Definition and Types of AI

Â Understanding artificial intelligence (AI) is crucial for its effective integration into education. AI refers to the simulation of human intelligence processes by machines, particularly computer systems. These processes include learning (the acquisition of information and rules for using it), reasoning (using rules to reach approximate or definite conclusions), and self-correction. In the context of education, AI can transform traditional learning paradigms, enabling personalized educational experiences that cater to individual student needs.

Â AI can be categorized into several types based on its capabilities and functionalities. The two primary classifications are narrow AI and general AI. Narrow

AI, also known as weak AI, is designed to perform a specific task or a limited range of tasks. Examples include virtual tutors that provide assistance in subjects like mathematics or language learning applications that adapt to a student's proficiency level. These systems excel in their designated functions but lack the ability to perform outside their programmed parameters.

In contrast, general AI, or strong AI, refers to machines that possess the ability to understand, learn, and apply knowledge across a wide array of tasks at a level comparable to human intelligence. While this type of AI remains largely theoretical at present, its potential implications for education are profound—envisioning an environment where students interact with intelligent systems capable of facilitating complex problem-solving and critical thinking skills.

Another important classification is based on machine learning techniques used within AI systems. This includes supervised learning, where algorithms learn from labeled data; unsupervised learning, which identifies patterns in unlabeled data; and reinforcement learning, where agents learn through trial-and-error interactions with their environment. Each method offers unique advantages for educational applications: supervised learning can enhance assessment tools while reinforcement learning can create adaptive learning environments that evolve based on student performance.

Â The integration of these various types of AI into educational frameworks not only supports individualized instruction but also fosters lifelong learning opportunities beyond traditional classroom settings. As educators embrace these technologies alongside their teaching methodologies, they pave the way for a more dynamic and responsive educational landscape.

2.2 Role of AI in Personalized Learning

Â The role of artificial intelligence (AI) in personalized learning is pivotal, as it enables educational experiences tailored to the unique needs and preferences of each student. This approach not only enhances engagement but also improves learning outcomes by addressing individual strengths and weaknesses. By leveraging data analytics and machine learning algorithms, AI systems can create customized learning paths that adapt in real-time to a student's progress.

 One significant aspect of AI-driven personalized learning is its ability to analyze vast amounts of data from various sources, including assessments, interactions with educational content, and even behavioral patterns. For instance, platforms like DreamBox Learning utilize adaptive algorithms to assess a student's understanding continuously. As students work through math problems, the system adjusts the difficulty level based on their performance, ensuring they are neither bored with tasks that are too easy nor overwhelmed by those that are too challenging.

 Moreover, AI can facilitate differentiated instruction by providing educators with insights into each student's learning style and pace. Tools such as intelligent tutoring systems offer recommendations for instructional strategies tailored to individual learners. For example, if a student struggles with visual-spatial reasoning in geometry, the system might suggest additional resources or alternative teaching methods focused on hands-on activities or interactive simulations.

Â Another critical benefit of AI in personalized learning is its capacity for continuous feedback. Unlike traditional assessment methods that often provide results after a delay, AI systems can deliver immediate feedback on quizzes and assignments. This instant response allows students to identify areas needing improvement promptly and encourages a growth mindset where mistakes become opportunities for learning rather than setbacks.

Â Furthermore, AI fosters inclusivity by accommodating diverse learner needs. Students with disabilities can benefit from personalized tools designed to support their specific challengesâ€"such as speech recognition software for those with writing difficulties or customized reading programs for individuals with dyslexia. These technologies ensure that all students have equitable access to quality education.

Â In conclusion, the integration of AI into personalized learning environments represents a transformative shift in education. By harnessing data-driven insights and adaptive technologies, educators can create more engaging and effective learning experiences that cater specifically to each student's journey.

2.3 Ethical Considerations in AI Implementation

Â The integration of artificial intelligence (AI) into educational settings brings forth a myriad of ethical considerations that must be addressed to ensure responsible implementation. As AI systems increasingly influence learning experiences, it is crucial to examine the implications of data privacy, algorithmic bias, and the potential for dehumanization in education.

Â One of the foremost ethical concerns is **data privacy**. AI systems rely heavily on data collection to function effectively, often gathering sensitive information about students' academic performance, behavioral patterns, and even personal details. This raises questions about who has access to this data and how it is used. Educational institutions must establish robust policies that protect student information from unauthorized access and misuse while ensuring compliance with regulations such as the Family

Educational Rights and Privacy Act (FERPA) in the United States.

Â **Algorithmic bias** presents another significant challenge. AI algorithms are only as good as the data they are trained on; if this data reflects societal biasesâ€"whether related to race, gender, or socioeconomic statusâ€"the resulting AI applications may perpetuate these inequalities. For instance, an intelligent tutoring system might inadvertently favor students from certain backgrounds if its training data lacks diversity. To mitigate this risk, developers must prioritize fairness in their algorithms by employing diverse datasets and conducting regular audits to identify and rectify biases.

Â The potential for **dehumanization** in education also warrants careful consideration. While AI can enhance personalized learning experiences, there is a risk that over-reliance on technology could diminish human interaction between educators and students. The role of teachers extends beyond mere content delivery; they provide emotional support and mentorship that cannot be replicated by machines. Therefore, it is essential to strike a balance where AI serves as a tool to augment teaching rather than replace the invaluable human elements of education.

 In conclusion, addressing these ethical considerations is vital for fostering trust among educators, students, and parents regarding AI's role in education. By prioritizing data privacy, combating algorithmic bias, and preserving human connections within learning environments, stakeholders can harness the benefits of AI while safeguarding against its potential pitfalls.

3

The Role of Teachers in an AI-Driven Classroom

3.1 Transitioning Teacher Roles

Â The transition of teacher roles in an AI-driven classroom is pivotal to reshaping the educational landscape. As artificial intelligence takes on more instructional responsibilities, teachers are evolving from traditional knowledge dispensers to facilitators and guides in a personalized learning environment. This shift not only enhances student autonomy but also redefines the essential skills that educators must cultivate to thrive in this new paradigm.

Â In this context, teachers will increasingly focus on developing critical thinking, creativity, and emotional intelligence among students. Rather than delivering lectures, they will engage learners through project-based activities that encourage collaboration and problem-solving. For instance, a teacher might facilitate a group project where students use AI tools to research environmental issues, guiding them in formulating questions and analyzing data rather than simply providing answers.

Â Moreover, the role of assessment will transform significantly. Teachers will need to adopt formative assessment techniques that leverage AI analytics to monitor student progress continuously. By interpreting data generated by AI systems, educators can identify individual learning gaps and tailor interventions accordingly. This proactive approach allows for timely support and fosters a growth mindset among students as they receive feedback based on their unique learning trajectories.

Â Additionally, professional development becomes crucial as teachers adapt to these new roles. Continuous training programs focused on integrating technology into pedagogy will empower educators with the necessary skills to navigate AI tools effectively. Schools may implement mentorship models where experienced teachers share best practices for utilizing AI resources while maintaining meaningful human connections with students.

Â Ultimately, transitioning teacher roles in an AI-driven classroom signifies a profound cultural shift within education. It emphasizes collaboration over competition and nurtures lifelong learning habits among both students and educators alike. As teachers embrace their evolving responsibilities, they become instrumental in guiding learners through an increasingly complex world shaped by technology.

3.2 Collaboration Between Teachers and AI

Â The collaboration between teachers and artificial intelligence (AI) represents a transformative shift in educational practices, enhancing the learning experience for students while redefining the role of educators. This partnership is not merely about integrating technology into classrooms; it is about creating a synergistic relationship where both teachers and AI contribute their unique strengths to foster an enriched learning environment.

Â One of the most significant aspects of this collaboration is the ability of AI to handle repetitive tasks, allowing teachers to focus on more complex pedagogical responsibilities. For instance, AI can automate administrative duties such as grading quizzes or tracking attendance, which frees up valuable time for educators to engage in meaningful interactions with students. This shift enables teachers to dedicate their efforts toward personalized instruction, mentoring, and fostering critical thinking skills among learners.

Â Moreover, AI systems can analyze vast amounts of data regarding student performance and learning patterns. By leveraging these insights, teachers can tailor their instructional strategies to meet individual needs effectively. For example, if an AI tool identifies that a particular student struggles with specific math concepts, the teacher can intervene with targeted support or resources designed to address those gaps. This data-driven approach not only enhances academic outcomes but also promotes a culture of continuous improvement within the classroom.

Â Collaboration also extends beyond individual classrooms; it encourages professional development among educators. Teachers can share best practices for utilizing AI tools through collaborative platforms or professional learning communities. Such environments foster innovation as educators experiment with different methods of integrating technology into their teaching while receiving feedback from peers who are navigating similar challenges.

Furthermore, this partnership cultivates a dynamic classroom atmosphere where students are encouraged to explore and interact with technology creatively. Teachers can guide students in using AI tools for research projects or problem-solving activities, promoting digital literacy alongside traditional academic skills. As students learn to navigate these technologies responsibly, they become better prepared for future careers in an increasingly tech-driven world.

In conclusion, the collaboration between teachers and AI is pivotal in reshaping educational landscapes by enhancing instructional effectiveness and fostering deeper student engagement. As this partnership evolves, it holds the potential to create more inclusive and adaptive learning environments that cater to diverse learner needs.

3.3 Professional Development for Educators

In an era where artificial intelligence (AI) is becoming increasingly integrated into educational settings, the professional development of educators is paramount. This development not only equips teachers with the necessary skills to effectively utilize AI tools but also fosters a mindset that embraces innovation and adaptability in teaching practices. As AI continues to evolve, so too must the competencies of educators who are tasked with guiding students through this technological landscape.

One critical aspect of professional development is the need for ongoing training that focuses on both technical proficiency and pedagogical strategies. Workshops and seminars should be designed to help educators understand how AI can enhance their teaching methods, such as using data analytics to inform instruction or employing adaptive learning technologies that cater to diverse student needs. For instance, a teacher might participate in a training session that demonstrates how to interpret AI-generated reports on student performance, enabling them to tailor their lessons more effectively.

Â Moreover, collaboration among educators plays a vital role in professional growth. Establishing communities of practice allows teachers to share experiences and best practices related to AI integration. These collaborative environments encourage experimentation and reflection, fostering a culture of continuous improvement. For example, teachers could engage in peer observations where they witness firsthand how colleagues implement AI tools in their classrooms, followed by discussions on successes and challenges faced during these implementations.

Â Additionally, mentorship programs can provide invaluable support for educators navigating the complexities of an AI-driven classroom. Experienced mentors can guide less experienced teachers through the nuances of integrating technology into their curricula while offering insights into effective classroom management strategies when utilizing AI resources. This relationship not only enhances individual teacher capabilities but also strengthens overall school culture by promoting shared learning experiences.

Â Ultimately, investing in comprehensive professional development ensures that educators are not merely passive users of technology but active participants in shaping its application within education. By prioritizing ongoing training and collaborative opportunities, schools can empower teachers to harness the full potential of AI, leading to enriched learning experiences for students and fostering an environment conducive to innovation.

4

Designing the AI Learning Environment

4.1 Infrastructure Requirements

Â The infrastructure requirements for an AI-driven learning environment are pivotal in facilitating a seamless transition from traditional educational systems to innovative, technology-enhanced models. This transformation not only necessitates robust technological frameworks but also demands a rethinking of physical and digital spaces where learning occurs. The integration of artificial intelligence into education requires careful planning and investment in various infrastructural components that support both educators and learners.

Â At the core of this infrastructure is the need for high-speed internet connectivity. Reliable access to the internet is essential for students to interact with AI systems, access online resources, and collaborate with peers globally. Schools must invest in advanced networking solutions that ensure consistent connectivity across all devices used by students and teachers alike. Furthermore, implementing cloud-based platforms can enhance accessibility, allowing learners to engage with educational materials anytime and anywhere.

Â In addition to connectivity, hardware plays a crucial role in supporting AI applications within the classroom. Classrooms should be equipped with modern computing devices such as laptops or tablets that can handle sophisticated software applications without lagging. Moreover, interactive tools like smartboards or augmented reality (AR) devices can enrich the learning experience by providing immersive environments where students can explore concepts dynamically.

Â Data management systems are another critical component of the infrastructure required for an AI learning environment. These systems must be capable of collecting, storing, and analyzing vast amounts of data generated by student interactions with AI tutors.

By leveraging big data analytics, educators can gain insights into individual learning patterns and adapt instructional strategies accordingly. Ensuring data privacy and security is paramount; thus, schools must implement stringent protocols to protect sensitive information.

Â Finally, professional development for educators is essential to maximize the potential of this new infrastructure. Teachers need training not only on how to use new technologies effectively but also on how to integrate AI tools into their pedagogical practices meaningfully. This holistic approach ensures that both technology and human expertise work synergistically to foster an enriching educational experience.

4.2 Integrating Technology into Classrooms

Â The integration of technology into classrooms is a transformative process that reshapes the educational landscape, enhancing both teaching and learning experiences. This shift not only involves the adoption of new tools but also necessitates a cultural change within educational institutions, where technology becomes an integral part of pedagogical practices. By leveraging various technological resources, educators can create dynamic learning environments that cater to diverse student needs and foster engagement.

 One significant aspect of integrating technology is the use of interactive platforms that facilitate collaboration among students. Tools such as Google Classroom or Microsoft Teams allow for real-time communication and project management, enabling students to work together seamlessly, regardless of their physical location. These platforms encourage peer-to-peer learning and help develop essential skills such as teamwork and digital literacy, which are crucial in today's workforce.

 Moreover, incorporating multimedia resources—such as videos, podcasts, and simulations—can significantly enhance comprehension and retention of complex concepts. For instance, using virtual reality (VR) applications allows students to immerse themselves in historical events or scientific phenomena, providing experiential learning opportunities that traditional methods cannot offer. Such immersive experiences can spark curiosity and motivate learners to explore subjects more deeply.

Additionally, personalized learning pathways enabled by adaptive technologies are revolutionizing how instruction is delivered. AI-driven tools can assess individual student performance in real-time and adjust content accordingly, ensuring that each learner progresses at their own pace. This tailored approach not only addresses varying skill levels but also promotes a sense of ownership over one's education.

 However, successful integration requires ongoing professional development for educators to ensure they are equipped with the necessary skills to utilize these technologies effectively. Training programs should focus on pedagogical strategies that incorporate technology meaningfully rather than merely using it as a substitute for traditional methods. By fostering a culture of continuous learning among teachers, schools can maximize the benefits of technological integration.

 In conclusion, integrating technology into classrooms is not just about adopting new tools; it involves rethinking educational practices to create engaging and effective learning environments. As schools embrace this transformation, they must prioritize collaboration, personalization, and professional growth to fully realize the potential of technology in education.

4.3 Creating Interactive Learning Spaces

Â Creating interactive learning spaces is essential for fostering an engaging and collaborative educational environment. These spaces not only enhance student participation but also promote critical thinking and creativity, which are vital skills in the modern world. By designing classrooms that encourage interaction, educators can facilitate deeper learning experiences that resonate with students on multiple levels.

Â One effective approach to creating interactive learning spaces is through the use of flexible seating arrangements. Traditional rows of desks can be replaced with various seating options such as bean bags, standing desks, or collaborative tables. This flexibility allows students to choose their preferred working environment, catering to different learning styles and promoting comfort. For instance, group work can be enhanced by arranging furniture in circles or clusters, encouraging dialogue and teamwork among peers.

Â Incorporating technology into these interactive spaces further amplifies engagement. Smart boards and interactive displays enable real-time collaboration during lessons, allowing students to contribute ideas visually and dynamically. Additionally, mobile devices can facilitate instant feedback through apps that allow students to respond to questions or participate in polls during class discussions. This immediate interaction not only keeps learners engaged but also provides teachers with valuable insights into student understanding.

Â Moreover, outdoor learning environments can serve as a unique extension of the classroom. Utilizing gardens or open spaces for hands-on activities encourages exploration and connection with nature while reinforcing curriculum concepts in a tangible way. For example, science classes can conduct experiments outdoors or engage in environmental studies directly within their surroundings, making learning more relevant and impactful.

Â Finally, fostering a culture of collaboration is crucial in these interactive spaces. Educators should encourage peer-to-peer teaching opportunities where students share knowledge and skills with one another. This not only builds confidence but also cultivates a sense of community within the classroom. By prioritizing interaction—whether through physical space design or collaborative practices—educators create vibrant learning environments that inspire curiosity and lifelong learning.

5

Curriculum Development for Lifelong Learning

5.1 Shifting from Traditional to Adaptive Curricula

 The transition from traditional curricula to adaptive curricula represents a pivotal shift in educational philosophy and practice. This transformation is essential for fostering lifelong learning, as it aligns educational experiences with the dynamic needs of learners in an ever-evolving world. Traditional education often relies on a one-size-fits-all approach, which can stifle creativity and fail to engage students meaningfully. In contrast, adaptive curricula leverage technology and personalized learning strategies to cater to individual student needs, preferences, and learning paces.

 Adaptive curricula utilize artificial intelligence (AI) and data analytics to create customized learning pathways for each student. For instance, platforms like **Khan Academy** or **Coursera** employ algorithms that assess a learner's progress and adjust content accordingly. This ensures that students are neither bored by material that is too easy nor overwhelmed by challenges that exceed their current capabilities. Such tailored approaches not only enhance engagement but also promote mastery of subjects through iterative learning processes.

Â The role of educators evolves significantly within this framework. Rather than being the primary source of knowledge, teachers become facilitators who guide students in navigating their personalized learning journeys. They provide support where needed while encouraging autonomy and self-directed exploration. This shift empowers students to take ownership of their education, fostering critical thinking skills and resilienceâ€"qualities essential for success in the 21st century.

Â Moreover, adaptive curricula extend beyond conventional classroom settings by promoting year-round learning opportunities. With access to online resources and flexible scheduling options, learners can pursue knowledge at their own pace throughout their lives. This continuous engagement with education helps individuals adapt to changing job markets and societal demands, ensuring they remain relevant in an increasingly competitive landscape.

Â In conclusion, the shift from traditional to adaptive curricula is not merely a technological upgrade; it represents a fundamental rethinking of how we approach education itself. By embracing this model, we can cultivate a generation of lifelong learners equipped with the skills necessary for personal fulfillment and professional success.

5.2 Incorporating Real-World Skills and Knowledge

Â The integration of real-world skills and knowledge into educational curricula is essential for preparing learners to navigate the complexities of modern life and work environments. This approach not only enhances the relevance of education but also fosters critical competencies that are increasingly demanded by employers and society at large. By embedding practical skills within academic frameworks, educators can create a more engaging and applicable learning experience.

 One effective strategy for incorporating real-world skills is through project-based learning (PBL). In PBL, students engage in hands-on projects that mirror real-life challenges, allowing them to apply theoretical knowledge in practical contexts. For instance, a high school science class might collaborate with local environmental organizations to conduct research on pollution levels in nearby water bodies. This not only teaches scientific principles but also instills teamwork, problem-solving, and communication skills—qualities that are invaluable in any career.

 Moreover, partnerships with local businesses and community organizations can enhance curriculum relevance. By involving industry professionals as guest speakers or mentors, students gain insights into current trends and expectations within various fields. Such collaborations can lead to internships or job shadowing opportunities that provide firsthand experience of workplace dynamics. For example, a business studies program could partner with local startups to allow students to develop marketing strategies for real products or services.

 Additionally, integrating technology into the curriculum plays a crucial role in bridging the gap between academic knowledge and practical application. Digital tools such as simulations, virtual labs, and online collaboration platforms enable learners to experiment with concepts in safe yet realistic environments. A computer science course might utilize coding boot camps or hackathons where students solve actual problems faced by tech companies, thereby enhancing their technical proficiency while fostering innovation.

 In conclusion, incorporating real-world skills and knowledge into curricula is vital for cultivating adaptable learners who are prepared for future challenges. By emphasizing experiential learning through projects, community partnerships, and technology integration, educational institutions can equip students with the necessary tools to thrive both personally and professionally in an ever-evolving landscape.

5.3 Continuous Curriculum Evaluation and Improvement

Continuous curriculum evaluation and improvement is a critical component of effective educational practices, ensuring that learning experiences remain relevant, engaging, and aligned with the evolving needs of students and society. This process involves systematic assessment of curriculum effectiveness through various methods, including feedback from stakeholders, performance metrics, and alignment with educational standards.

One essential aspect of continuous evaluation is the incorporation of stakeholder feedback. Engaging students, educators, parents, and industry professionals in discussions about curriculum content can provide valuable insights into its relevance and effectiveness. For instance, regular surveys or focus groups can be conducted to gather opinions on course materials and teaching methodologies. This participatory approach not only fosters a sense of ownership among stakeholders but also helps identify areas for enhancement that may not be apparent to educators alone.

Moreover, data-driven decision-making plays a pivotal role in curriculum improvement. By analyzing student performance data—such as grades, assessments, and standardized test scores—educators can pinpoint specific strengths and weaknesses within the curriculum. For example, if a significant number of students struggle with particular concepts in mathematics, this could indicate a need for revising instructional strategies or providing additional resources to support learning. Utilizing analytics tools can streamline this process by offering real-time insights into student progress.

 Another vital element is the integration of professional development for educators. Continuous improvement requires that teachers are equipped with the latest pedagogical strategies and subject knowledge. Ongoing training sessions focused on innovative teaching techniques or emerging technologies can empower educators to adapt their instruction effectively based on evaluation outcomes. For instance, workshops on differentiated instruction can help teachers tailor their approaches to meet diverse learner needs more effectively.

In conclusion, continuous curriculum evaluation and improvement is an ongoing cycle that enhances educational quality by incorporating stakeholder feedback, leveraging data analysis for informed decisions, and investing in teacher development. By committing to this iterative process, educational institutions can ensure that their curricula remain dynamic and responsive to the changing landscape of education.

6

Student-Centered Learning Approaches

6.1 Fostering Independence in Learners

Fostering independence in learners is a crucial aspect of modern education, particularly within the context of student-centered learning approaches. This shift emphasizes the importance of equipping students with the skills and mindset necessary to take charge of their own learning journeys. By nurturing independence, educators can help students develop critical thinking, problem-solving abilities, and self-motivation—qualities essential for lifelong learning.

One effective strategy for promoting learner independence is through personalized learning experiences. When students are given choices regarding their learning paths—such as selecting topics that interest them or determining how they wish to demonstrate their understanding—they become more engaged and invested in their education. For instance, a project-based approach allows students to explore real-world problems while applying their knowledge creatively. This autonomy not only enhances motivation but also encourages learners to take responsibility for their educational outcomes.

Additionally, integrating technology into the classroom can significantly support independent learning. Tools such as online resources, educational apps, and artificial intelligence-driven platforms provide students with access to a wealth of information and diverse perspectives. These technologies empower learners to seek answers independently while allowing teachers to act as facilitators rather than traditional sources of knowledge. For example, using AI tutors can help personalize instruction based on individual student needs, fostering an environment where learners feel confident exploring subjects at their own pace.

Moreover, teaching metacognitive strategies is vital in helping students reflect on their learning processes. Encouraging learners to set goals, monitor their progress, and evaluate outcomes cultivates self-awareness and critical reflection. Techniques such as journaling or peer discussions can facilitate this reflective practice, enabling students to identify strengths and areas for improvement actively.

Â In conclusion, fostering independence in learners is integral to creating a dynamic educational landscape that prepares individuals for future challenges. By implementing personalized learning experiences, leveraging technology effectively, and promoting metacognitive awareness, educators can cultivate independent thinkers who are equipped for lifelong success.

6.2 Encouraging Critical Thinking and Problem Solving

Â Encouraging critical thinking and problem-solving skills is essential in student-centered learning approaches, as these competencies empower learners to navigate complex challenges both in academic settings and real-world scenarios. By fostering an environment where questioning, analysis, and creativity are prioritized, educators can cultivate a generation of thinkers who are not only knowledgeable but also capable of applying their knowledge effectively.

One effective method for promoting critical thinking is through the use of inquiry-based learning. This approach encourages students to ask questions, conduct research, and engage in discussions that lead to deeper understanding. For instance, when students explore a scientific phenomenon by formulating hypotheses and conducting experiments, they learn to analyze data critically and draw conclusions based on evidence. This hands-on experience not only enhances their analytical skills but also instills a sense of curiosity that drives lifelong learning.

Moreover, integrating collaborative projects into the curriculum can significantly enhance problem-solving abilities. When students work together to tackle real-world issues—such as environmental sustainability or community health—they must communicate effectively, negotiate differing viewpoints, and synthesize diverse ideas. This collaborative process fosters teamwork while challenging students to think critically about solutions that consider multiple perspectives. For example, a group project focused on designing a sustainable garden requires students to research plant species, understand ecological principles, and develop practical implementation strategies.

Additionally, incorporating case studies into lessons provides students with opportunities to apply critical thinking in realistic contexts. Analyzing historical events or contemporary social issues allows learners to evaluate different viewpoints and assess the implications of various decisions. By engaging with complex scenarios that lack clear-cut answers, students develop the ability to weigh evidence critically and make informed judgments.

In conclusion, encouraging critical thinking and problem-solving within student-centered learning frameworks is vital for preparing learners for future challenges. Through inquiry-based learning, collaborative projects, and case study analyses, educators can create dynamic environments where students actively engage with content while developing essential skills for success beyond the classroom.

6.3 Supporting Diverse Learning Styles

Â Supporting diverse learning styles is a fundamental aspect of student-centered learning approaches, as it recognizes that each learner possesses unique preferences and strengths in how they acquire knowledge. By tailoring educational experiences to accommodate these differences, educators can enhance engagement, motivation, and overall academic success. This section explores various strategies for effectively supporting diverse learning styles within the classroom.

Â One effective method for addressing different learning styles is through differentiated instruction. This approach involves modifying content, processes, and products based on students' individual needs. For instance, visual learners may benefit from graphic organizers or videos that illustrate concepts visually, while auditory learners might thrive in environments where discussions and verbal explanations are emphasized. Kinesthetic learners often require hands-on activities to grasp abstract ideas; thus, incorporating experiments or role-playing scenarios can significantly enhance their understanding.

Additionally, employing technology can play a crucial role in catering to diverse learning preferences. Educational software and online resources offer interactive platforms that allow students to engage with material at their own pace. For example, platforms like Khan Academy provide video tutorials for visual learners alongside practice exercises for those who learn best through doing. Such tools not only support varied learning styles but also promote self-directed learning—a key component of student-centered education.

Moreover, fostering a collaborative classroom environment encourages peer-to-peer learning, which can be particularly beneficial for students with different learning styles. Group projects enable students to share their strengths; for instance, a student who excels in research can assist peers who may struggle with information synthesis. This collaborative dynamic not only reinforces content understanding but also builds essential social skills such as communication and teamwork.

In conclusion, supporting diverse learning styles is vital in creating an inclusive educational environment where all students can thrive. Through differentiated instruction, the integration of technology, and collaborative opportunities, educators can ensure that every learner's unique needs are met—ultimately leading to enhanced academic outcomes and personal growth.

7

Assessment and Evaluation in an AI Framework

7.1 Redefining Success Metrics

 In the context of an AI-driven educational framework, redefining success metrics is crucial for aligning assessment with the evolving nature of learning. Traditional metrics, such as standardized test scores and grade point averages, often fail to capture the depth of knowledge and skills that students acquire through personalized learning experiences facilitated by artificial intelligence. As education shifts towards a model where AI plays a central role in guiding student learning, it becomes imperative to establish new benchmarks that reflect this transformation.

 One significant aspect of redefining success metrics involves moving from quantitative assessments to qualitative evaluations. For instance, rather than solely relying on numerical grades, educators can incorporate portfolios showcasing a student's work over time. These portfolios can include projects, reflections, and peer feedback, providing a more holistic view of a learner's progress and capabilities. This shift encourages students to engage deeply with their learning material and fosters critical thinking skills.

Â Additionally, success metrics should encompass social-emotional learning (SEL) outcomes. In an AI-enhanced environment where collaboration is key, measuring interpersonal skills such as teamwork, communication, and empathy becomes essential. Tools like self-assessments or peer evaluations can be integrated into the evaluation process to gauge these competencies effectively. By prioritizing SEL alongside academic achievements, we prepare students not only for academic success but also for thriving in diverse social contexts.

Â Moreover, adaptive learning technologies provide real-time data on student engagement and understanding. Utilizing analytics from these platforms allows educators to tailor their teaching strategies based on individual performance trends rather than relying on periodic assessments alone. This continuous feedback loop enables timely interventions when students struggle or excel in specific areas.

Â Ultimately, redefining success metrics within an AI framework requires a comprehensive approach that values creativity, emotional intelligence, and lifelong learning habits over traditional measures of achievement. By embracing this broader perspective on success, we can cultivate learners who are not only knowledgeable but also adaptable and resilient in an ever-changing world.

7.2 Formative vs Summative Assessments

Â Understanding the distinction between formative and summative assessments is essential in an AI-driven educational framework, as each serves a unique purpose in the learning process. Formative assessments are ongoing evaluations that provide feedback during the learning journey, while summative assessments occur at the end of an instructional period to evaluate overall learning outcomes. This differentiation is crucial for educators aiming to leverage AI tools effectively to enhance student learning.

Â Formative assessments are designed to monitor student progress and inform instruction. They can take various forms, including quizzes, discussions, peer reviews, and interactive activities facilitated by AI platforms. For instance, adaptive learning technologies can analyze student responses in real-time, allowing educators to adjust their teaching strategies based on individual performance trends. This immediate feedback loop not only helps identify areas where students may struggle but also fosters a growth mindset by encouraging continuous improvement.

Â In contrast, summative assessments aim to measure what students have learned at a specific point in time. These assessments often include final exams, standardized tests, or major projects that encapsulate the knowledge gained over a course or unit. While they provide valuable data on overall achievement levels and program effectiveness, relying solely on summative assessments can overlook critical aspects of student development that occur throughout the learning process.

Â The integration of AI into both formative and summative assessment practices offers opportunities for innovation. For example, AI can help create personalized assessment experiences that adapt to individual learner needs in formative contexts while also analyzing large datasets from summative assessments to identify trends across different demographics or educational settings. This dual approach ensures that both types of assessment contribute meaningfully to understanding student progress and success.

Â Ultimately, balancing formative and summative assessments within an AI framework allows educators to cultivate a more comprehensive view of student learning. By prioritizing ongoing feedback alongside final evaluations, we can better support learners' diverse needs and prepare them for future challenges in an increasingly complex world.

7.3 Utilizing Data Analytics for Student Progress

Â The integration of data analytics in education has transformed the way educators assess and understand student progress. By harnessing vast amounts of data generated through various learning activities, institutions can gain insights that were previously unattainable. This capability not only enhances the educational experience but also allows for a more tailored approach to teaching and learning.

Â Data analytics enables educators to track individual student performance over time, identifying trends and patterns that inform instructional strategies. For instance, by analyzing quiz results, participation rates in discussions, and assignment submissions, teachers can pinpoint specific areas where students excel or struggle. This granular view of student progress facilitates timely interventions, ensuring that no learner falls behind. Moreover, predictive analytics can forecast future performance based on historical data, allowing educators to proactively address potential challenges before they escalate.

Â Furthermore, the use of dashboards powered by AI can present real-time data visualizations that make it easier for educators to interpret complex datasets. These dashboards often include metrics such as engagement levels, completion rates, and mastery of key concepts. By providing a comprehensive overview at a glance, educators can make informed decisions about curriculum adjustments or targeted support initiatives aimed at enhancing student outcomes.

In addition to supporting individual learners, data analytics fosters collaboration among educators by enabling them to share insights and best practices derived from collective experiences. Schools can establish professional learning communities where teachers discuss findings from their analyses and collaborate on strategies to improve overall student achievement across different demographics.

 Ultimately, utilizing data analytics for monitoring student progress not only enriches the educational landscape but also empowers both students and teachers. As educational institutions continue to embrace these technologies, they pave the way for a more personalized learning environment that adapts to the unique needs of each learner while fostering continuous improvement in teaching methodologies.

8

Year-Round Learning Models

8.1 Benefits of Continuous Education

Â The concept of continuous education is pivotal in reshaping the educational landscape, particularly within a year-round learning model. This approach not only fosters lifelong learning but also equips individuals with the skills necessary to adapt to an ever-evolving job market. As technology advances and industries transform, the need for ongoing education becomes increasingly critical.

Â One significant benefit of continuous education is its ability to enhance employability. In a world where job requirements are constantly changing, individuals who engage in lifelong learning can stay relevant and competitive. For instance, professionals in fields such as technology or healthcare must regularly update their knowledge and skills to keep pace with innovations and regulatory changes. By participating in continuous education programs, they can ensure that their expertise remains current, thereby increasing their value to employers.

Â Moreover, continuous education promotes personal growth and development. Engaging in new learning experiences can lead to increased confidence and self-esteem as individuals master new skills or concepts. This personal enrichment often translates into greater job satisfaction and overall well-being. For example, someone who takes up courses in public speaking may find not only career advancement opportunities but also improved communication skills that enhance their personal relationships.

Â Another advantage is the fostering of a culture of curiosity and innovation. When educational systems encourage year-round learning, they create environments where questioning and exploration are valued. This shift can lead to more creative problem-solving approaches within organizations as employees feel empowered to think outside the box. Companies that support continuous education often see higher levels of employee engagement and retention because workers feel invested in their professional development.

Â Lastly, continuous education facilitates networking opportunities among learners from diverse backgrounds. These interactions can lead to collaborations that drive innovation across various sectors. By connecting with peers through workshops or online courses, individuals expand their professional networks while gaining insights from different perspectives.

8.2 Structuring Flexible Learning Schedules

Â In the context of year-round learning models, structuring flexible learning schedules is essential for accommodating diverse learner needs and maximizing educational outcomes. This approach recognizes that traditional academic calendars may not suit everyone, particularly in a rapidly changing world where personal and professional commitments vary widely.

Â One of the primary advantages of flexible learning schedules is their ability to cater to individual learning paces. For instance, adult learners often juggle work and family responsibilities alongside their education.

By offering courses that can be taken at various times throughout the year, institutions enable these learners to engage with material when it best fits their lives. This flexibility can lead to higher retention rates and improved academic performance as students are less likely to feel overwhelmed by rigid deadlines.

Â Moreover, incorporating asynchronous learning options into flexible schedules allows students to access course materials at their convenience. This model not only supports different time zones but also accommodates varying levels of technological proficiency among learners. For example, a student working full-time may prefer evening or weekend classes, while another might thrive in an entirely online format that allows them to learn at their own pace without the constraints of a fixed timetable.

Â Additionally, structuring flexible schedules encourages interdisciplinary learning opportunities. By allowing students to mix and match courses from different fields throughout the year, educational institutions can foster a more holistic understanding of complex subjects. For instance, a student interested in environmental science could take courses in policy-making during one term and then switch focus to renewable energy technologies in another, creating a richer educational experience.

Â Finally, effective communication about available scheduling options is crucial for maximizing participation in flexible programs. Institutions should actively promote these offerings through targeted outreach efforts that highlight how such structures can meet diverse learner needs. By doing so, they not only enhance enrollment but also cultivate an inclusive educational environment where all students feel empowered to pursue lifelong learning.

8.3 Balancing Academic and Personal Growth

Â In the realm of year-round learning models, achieving a balance between academic pursuits and personal growth is paramount. This equilibrium not only enhances educational outcomes but also fosters well-rounded individuals who are prepared for the complexities of modern life. The integration of academic rigor with opportunities for personal development creates an environment where learners can thrive both intellectually and emotionally.

One significant aspect of this balance is the recognition that education extends beyond traditional classroom settings. For instance, experiential learning opportunities such as internships, community service, and study abroad programs allow students to apply their knowledge in real-world contexts. These experiences cultivate essential skills like critical thinking, adaptability, and interpersonal communication—qualities that are increasingly valued in today's job market. By incorporating these elements into year-round learning schedules, institutions can support students in developing a holistic skill set.

Moreover, fostering a culture that prioritizes mental health and well-being is crucial for maintaining this balance. Educational institutions should implement wellness programs that encourage self-care practices among students. Activities such as mindfulness workshops, physical fitness classes, or creative arts sessions can provide necessary breaks from academic pressures while promoting emotional resilience. When students feel supported in their personal lives, they are more likely to excel academically.

Â Additionally, mentorship plays a vital role in bridging academic goals with personal aspirations. Establishing mentorship programs where experienced professionals guide students can help them navigate both their educational paths and career choices effectively. Mentors can offer insights into balancing work-life commitments while pursuing academic excellence, thus equipping students with strategies to manage their time efficiently.

Â Ultimately, the synergy between academic achievement and personal growth leads to lifelong learners who are not only knowledgeable but also adaptable and empathetic individuals ready to contribute positively to society. By embracing this dual focus within year-round learning models, educational institutions can create enriching environments that prepare students for success on multiple fronts.

9

Community Involvement and Support Systems

9.1 Engaging Parents and Guardians

Â Engaging parents and guardians is a critical component in the transformation of the educational landscape, particularly as we shift towards an AI-guided learning model. Their involvement not only enhances student motivation but also fosters a collaborative environment that bridges home and school. In this new paradigm, where students are encouraged to take charge of their own learning with the assistance of artificial intelligence, parents play an essential role in supporting this journey.

Â One effective strategy for engaging parents is through regular communication that emphasizes the benefits of AI-assisted education. Schools can host workshops or informational sessions that demystify how AI tools work and illustrate their potential to personalize learning experiences. For instance, showcasing success stories from other families who have embraced this approach can inspire confidence and enthusiasm among hesitant parents.

Â Moreover, creating platforms for ongoing dialogue between educators and families is vital. Utilizing digital communication tools such as apps or online portals allows parents to track their child's progress in real-time, fostering transparency and accountability. This engagement can be further enhanced by encouraging feedback from parents about their children's experiences with AI learning systems, which can help educators refine their approaches based on community input.

- Establishing parent-teacher committees focused on technology integration can empower guardians to voice concerns and contribute ideas.
- Offering flexible meeting times ensures that all parents have the opportunity to participate in discussions about their child's education.

- Creating resource guides that outline how parents can support their children's independent learning at home reinforces the partnership between school and family.

 Ultimately, fostering a culture of engagement requires schools to recognize parents as partners in education rather than mere observers. By actively involving them in the transition towards an AI-enhanced educational system, we create a supportive network that not only benefits students but also strengthens community ties. This holistic approach ensures that every stakeholder feels valued and invested in the lifelong learning journey ahead.

9.2 Building Partnerships with Local Organizations

 Building partnerships with local organizations is a vital strategy for enhancing community involvement in educational initiatives. These collaborations not only provide additional resources and support but also create a network of shared goals that can significantly enrich the learning environment for students. By leveraging the strengths of local organizations, schools can foster a more integrated approach to education that benefits both students and the wider community.

One effective way to establish these partnerships is through outreach programs that identify potential collaborators within the community. Schools can engage with local businesses, non-profits, and cultural institutions to explore mutual interests and objectives. For instance, a local library might partner with a school to offer after-school tutoring sessions or reading programs, thereby extending learning opportunities beyond the classroom. Such initiatives not only enhance student engagement but also promote literacy and lifelong learning within the community.

  Moreover, involving local organizations in curriculum development can lead to more relevant and practical educational experiences. By integrating real-world applications into lessons—such as inviting professionals from various fields to share their expertise—students gain insights into potential career paths while developing essential skills. This approach not only enriches academic content but also helps students understand the value of their education in relation to community needs.

  Additionally, fostering these partnerships requires ongoing communication and collaboration. Schools should establish regular meetings with organizational partners to assess progress, share feedback, and adapt strategies as necessary. Utilizing digital platforms for communication can facilitate this process by allowing stakeholders to stay connected and informed about each other's activities.

- Creating joint events such as career fairs or community service days can strengthen ties between schools and local organizations.
- Encouraging volunteerism among staff members at local organizations fosters goodwill and enhances relationships.
- Developing internship or mentorship programs through these partnerships provides students with valuable hands-on experience.

Â Ultimately, building strong partnerships with local organizations cultivates a sense of shared responsibility for education within the community. By working together towards common goals, schools and organizations can create an enriched educational landscape that supports student success while addressing broader societal challenges.

9.3 Creating Support Networks for Students

 Creating support networks for students is essential in fostering an environment where they can thrive academically, socially, and emotionally. These networks not only provide a safety net for students facing challenges but also enhance their overall educational experience by promoting collaboration and community engagement.

 One of the most effective ways to establish these support networks is through peer mentoring programs. By pairing older or more experienced students with younger ones, schools can create a culture of guidance and encouragement. This relationship allows mentees to receive personalized advice on academic subjects, social issues, and even college preparation. For instance, high school seniors could mentor freshmen, helping them navigate the transition into a new environment while building lasting friendships that contribute to a sense of belonging.

 In addition to peer mentoring, schools should consider involving parents and guardians in the support network. Parent-teacher associations (PTAs) can play a pivotal role in creating forums where families can share resources and strategies for supporting their children's education. Workshops on topics such as study skills or mental health awareness can empower parents to be active participants in their children's learning journey. Furthermore, establishing communication channels between teachers and families ensures that everyone is aligned in supporting student success.

 Community organizations also serve as vital components of student support networks. Schools can collaborate with local nonprofits that focus on youth development or mental health services to provide additional resources for students in need. For example, partnerships with counseling centers can offer workshops on stress management or conflict resolution directly within the school setting, making these services more accessible to students who may otherwise hesitate to seek help.

 Finally, leveraging technology can enhance these support systems significantly. Online platforms dedicated to student engagement allow for virtual mentorship opportunities and resource sharing among peers across different schools or communities. Social media groups focused on academic subjects or extracurricular interests enable students to connect with like-minded individuals who share similar goals and challenges.

Ultimately, creating robust support networks requires intentionality and collaboration among all stakeholders—students, educators, families, and community members alike—to cultivate an inclusive atmosphere that champions student well-being and success.

10

Addressing Equity and Accessibility Issues

10.1 Ensuring Equal Access to Technology

 Ensuring equal access to technology is a fundamental pillar in the transition towards an educational system that leverages artificial intelligence for personalized learning. In a world increasingly driven by digital tools, disparities in access can exacerbate existing inequalities, hindering students' ability to thrive in this new paradigm. This section explores the critical importance of equitable technology access and its implications for lifelong learning.

 The digital divide remains a pressing issue, particularly in underserved communities where students may lack reliable internet connectivity or access to modern devices. For instance, during the

COVID-19 pandemic, many schools shifted to online learning; however, students from low-income families faced significant challenges due to inadequate resources. Addressing these gaps is essential not only for immediate educational outcomes but also for fostering long-term equity in opportunities.

 To combat these disparities, initiatives must be implemented at multiple levels. Schools and governments should collaborate with tech companies to provide affordable devices and subsidized internet services. Programs like **One Laptop per Child** have shown promise by distributing low-cost laptops to children in developing regions, enabling them to engage with digital content effectively. Such efforts can empower students by equipping them with the necessary tools for independent learning guided by AI.

 Moreover, teacher training plays a crucial role in ensuring that all students benefit from technological advancements. Educators must be equipped not only with the skills to use technology effectively but also with strategies to support diverse learners who may face unique challenges when engaging with digital platforms. Professional development programs should emphasize inclusive teaching practices that leverage technology as a means of enhancing accessibility.

Â Finally, community involvement is vital in promoting equal access to technology. Local organizations can facilitate workshops that educate families about available resources and how best to utilize them for their children's education. By fostering partnerships between schools, families, and community groups, we can create a supportive ecosystem that champions equitable access and empowers every student on their educational journey.

10.2 Strategies for Inclusive Education

Â Inclusive education is essential for fostering a learning environment where all students, regardless of their backgrounds or abilities, can thrive. This approach not only promotes equity but also enriches the educational experience by embracing diversity. Implementing effective strategies for inclusive education requires a multifaceted approach that addresses various aspects of teaching and learning.

Â One critical strategy is the adoption of Universal Design for Learning (UDL), which emphasizes flexible methods of engagement, representation, and action/expression. By designing curricula that accommodate diverse learning styles and needs from the outset, educators can create an environment where every student has equal opportunities to succeed. For instance, incorporating multimedia resources can cater to visual and auditory learners simultaneously, while providing options for students to demonstrate their understanding through different formats—such as presentations, written reports, or creative projects—can empower them to express their knowledge in ways that resonate with them.

Another vital component is fostering a culture of collaboration among educators, support staff, families, and the community. Professional development programs should focus on equipping teachers with skills in co-teaching models and differentiated instruction techniques. Collaborative teaching allows educators to share expertise and provide tailored support to students with varying needs within the same classroom setting. Additionally, involving families in the educational process ensures that they are informed partners in their children's learning journey; schools can host workshops that educate parents about inclusive practices and how they can reinforce these at home.

Â Moreover, leveraging technology plays a significant role in enhancing inclusivity. Assistive technologies such as speech-to-text software or interactive applications can help bridge gaps for students with disabilities or those who require additional support. Schools should invest in training teachers on how to effectively integrate these tools into their lessons while ensuring accessibility features are utilized across all digital platforms.

Â Finally, continuous assessment and feedback mechanisms are crucial for monitoring progress and making necessary adjustments to instructional strategies. Regularly gathering input from students about their experiences fosters an inclusive atmosphere where they feel valued and heard. By implementing these strategies holistically, educational institutions can create environments that not only accommodate but celebrate diversity among learners.

10.3 Overcoming Barriers to Participation

Â Overcoming barriers to participation is crucial for ensuring that all individuals, particularly those from marginalized groups, can engage fully in educational settings and community activities. These barriers can be physical, social, or systemic, and addressing them requires a comprehensive understanding of the challenges faced by diverse populations.

Â One significant barrier is the lack of accessible infrastructure. Many educational institutions are not equipped with facilities that accommodate students with disabilities. This includes inadequate ramps, elevators, or accessible restrooms. To combat this issue, schools must conduct thorough accessibility audits and invest in necessary renovations to create an inclusive environment. For instance, implementing tactile pathways for visually impaired students or providing adjustable desks for wheelchair users can significantly enhance participation.

Â Social stigma also plays a critical role in hindering participation. Students with disabilities or those from minority backgrounds may face discrimination or bullying, which discourages them from engaging fully in school activities. To address this challenge, fostering a culture of acceptance and respect within educational institutions is essential. Programs that promote diversity awareness and empathy among students can help dismantle stereotypes and encourage supportive peer relationships.

Â Moreover, systemic barriers such as rigid curricula and assessment methods often exclude non-traditional learners. Educational systems should adopt flexible teaching strategies that cater to various learning styles and needs. For example, incorporating project-based learning allows students to demonstrate their knowledge through creative means rather than standardized tests alone. This approach not only accommodates different abilities but also fosters collaboration among peers.

Â Finally, active involvement of families and communities is vital in overcoming these barriers. Schools should establish partnerships with local organizations that support underrepresented groups to provide resources and advocacy for families navigating the education system. Workshops aimed at educating parents about their rights and available support services can empower them to advocate effectively for their children's needs.

 By addressing these multifaceted barriers through targeted strategies—ranging from infrastructural improvements to cultural shifts—educational institutions can create environments where every individual has the opportunity to participate meaningfully.

11

Global Perspectives on AI in Education

11.1 Case Studies from Around the World

Â The integration of artificial intelligence (AI) in education is not merely a theoretical concept; it is being actively implemented across various countries, showcasing diverse approaches and outcomes. These case studies illustrate how AI can transform educational practices, enhance learning experiences, and prepare students for a rapidly evolving job market.

Â In Finland, known for its progressive education system, AI has been incorporated into personalized learning environments. Schools utilize AI-driven platforms that assess individual student performance and adapt curricula accordingly. This approach allows teachers to focus on facilitating discussions and providing emotional support rather than traditional lecturing. The results have shown improved student engagement and academic performance, demonstrating the potential of AI to complement human instruction effectively.

Meanwhile, in India, initiatives like the "Smart Learning" program leverage AI to address educational disparities in rural areas. By using mobile applications powered by AI algorithms, students gain access to quality educational resources that were previously unavailable. These tools provide interactive lessons tailored to each student's learning pace, significantly improving literacy rates among children who would otherwise lack access to formal education.

In the United States, universities are experimenting with AI chatbots designed to assist students with administrative tasks and academic inquiries. For instance, Georgia State University implemented an AI chatbot named "Pounce," which has successfully reduced dropout rates by providing timely information about course registration and financial aid options. This case highlights how AI can streamline processes within educational institutions while enhancing student support services.

These global case studies underscore the multifaceted role of AI in education—ranging from personalized learning experiences to administrative efficiencies—while also highlighting challenges that must be navigated as these technologies become more prevalent.

Lastly, in China, the use of facial recognition technology in classrooms has sparked both interest and controversy. Some schools employ this technology to monitor student engagement levels during lessons. While proponents argue that it helps identify students who may need additional support or motivation, critics raise concerns about privacy issues and the ethical implications of surveillance in educational settings.

11.2 Lessons Learned from International Practices

The integration of artificial intelligence (AI) in education across various countries has yielded valuable lessons that can inform future implementations. These insights not only highlight the potential benefits of AI but also underscore the challenges and ethical considerations that must be addressed to ensure equitable access and effective learning outcomes.

Â One significant lesson is the importance of context-specific solutions. For instance, while Finland's approach emphasizes personalized learning through AI-driven platforms, this model may not be directly applicable in regions with limited technological infrastructure. In India, the "Smart Learning" initiative demonstrates how mobile applications can bridge educational gaps in rural areas by providing tailored content. This adaptability underscores the necessity for educational technologies to align with local needs and resources.

Â Another critical insight is the role of teacher training and support in successful AI integration. In many cases, educators are at the forefront of implementing these technologies; thus, their comfort and proficiency with AI tools are paramount. Countries like Singapore have invested heavily in professional development programs that equip teachers with the skills needed to leverage AI effectively in their classrooms. This investment not only enhances teaching practices but also fosters a culture of innovation within schools.

Â Moreover, ethical considerations surrounding data privacy and surveillance have emerged as pivotal themes in discussions about AI in education. The use of facial recognition technology in Chinese classrooms raises questions about student consent and privacy rights. As educational institutions adopt more sophisticated technologies, it is essential to establish clear guidelines that protect students' personal information while still allowing for beneficial data usage.

 Finally, fostering collaboration among stakeholders—governments, educators, technologists, and communities—is crucial for creating sustainable AI initiatives in education. Successful examples from around the world illustrate that when diverse perspectives come together, they can develop comprehensive strategies that address both technological advancements and social equity issues.

11.3 Adapting Global Innovations Locally

 The adaptation of global innovations in artificial intelligence (AI) for local educational contexts is crucial for maximizing their effectiveness and ensuring equitable access to learning opportunities. As countries increasingly look to integrate AI technologies into their educational systems, understanding how to tailor these innovations to meet local needs becomes paramount. This process not only involves technological adjustments but also cultural, social, and infrastructural considerations that can significantly influence the success of AI initiatives.

 One key aspect of adapting global innovations locally is recognizing the diverse educational landscapes across different regions. For instance, while AI-driven platforms may thrive in urban settings with robust internet connectivity, rural areas may require offline solutions or mobile-based applications that function without constant internet access. The "Smart Learning" initiative in India exemplifies this approach by utilizing mobile technology to deliver personalized content tailored to the unique challenges faced by students in remote locations.

 Moreover, engaging local stakeholders—such as educators, parents, and community leaders—in the adaptation process is essential. Their insights can provide valuable context regarding cultural norms and specific educational needs that might not be apparent from a global perspective. Collaborative efforts can lead to the co-creation of AI tools that resonate more deeply with local users, thereby enhancing acceptance and usage rates among both teachers and students.

Â Additionally, training programs must be designed with local realities in mind. In many cases, teachers are expected to implement new technologies without adequate preparation or support. Countries like Singapore have demonstrated success by investing in professional development tailored specifically for educators' needs related to AI integration. Such initiatives ensure that teachers feel confident using these tools effectively within their classrooms.

Â Finally, ethical considerations surrounding data privacy must be addressed when adapting global innovations locally. Different regions have varying regulations regarding data protection; thus, it is vital for educational institutions to establish clear guidelines that respect local laws while still leveraging data for improved learning outcomes. By prioritizing ethical practices alongside innovative solutions, stakeholders can foster trust and promote a sustainable future for AI in education.

12

Future Trends in Educational Technology

12.1 Emerging Technologies Impacting Education

Â The integration of emerging technologies in education is reshaping the landscape of learning, making it more personalized, accessible, and engaging. As we transition from traditional educational models to innovative frameworks, these technologies play a crucial role in facilitating lifelong learning and fostering independent knowledge acquisition among students.

Â One of the most significant advancements is the use of **artificial intelligence (AI)**Knewton utilize adaptive learning algorithms to provide customized content recommendations based on real-time data analysis. This not only enhances student engagement but also empowers learners to take control of their educational journeys.

Â **Virtual reality (VR)** and **augmented reality (AR)** are also making waves in education by creating immersive learning environments that transcend traditional classroom boundaries. These technologies allow students to explore complex subjects through interactive simulations and visualizations. For example, medical students can practice surgical procedures in a risk-free VR environment, while history classes can take virtual field trips to ancient civilizations, enriching their understanding through experiential learning.

Â The rise of **blockchain technology** presents another transformative opportunity for education by enhancing credential verification processes and ensuring secure record-keeping. Institutions can leverage blockchain to issue tamper-proof diplomas and certificates, streamlining the hiring process for employers who seek verified qualifications. This innovation not only increases trust in academic credentials but also promotes transparency within the educational system.

Â Finally, the proliferation of **online collaborative tools**, such as Google Workspace or Microsoft Teams, fosters a culture of teamwork and communication among students regardless of geographical barriers. These platforms enable real-time collaboration on projects and assignments, preparing students for a globalized workforce where remote work is increasingly common.

Â Together, these emerging technologies are not just enhancing existing educational practices; they are fundamentally redefining what it means to learn in the 21st century. As educators embrace these innovations, they pave the way for a more dynamic and inclusive approach to education that prioritizes student agency and continuous growth.

12.2 Predictions for the Next Decade

Â The next decade promises to be a transformative period for educational technology, driven by rapid advancements in various fields. As we look ahead, several key trends are expected to shape the future of learning environments, making education more inclusive, efficient, and engaging.

Â One significant prediction is the widespread adoption of **artificial intelligence (AI)** across educational institutions. AI will not only personalize learning experiences but also automate administrative tasks, allowing educators to focus more on teaching and mentoring students. For instance, intelligent tutoring systems could provide real-time feedback and support tailored to individual student needs, enhancing their learning outcomes. Furthermore, AI-driven analytics will enable institutions to identify at-risk students early on and implement timely interventions.

Â **Virtual reality (VR)** and **augmented reality (AR)** technologies are anticipated to become mainstream tools in classrooms. These immersive technologies will facilitate experiential learning by simulating real-world scenarios that enhance understanding and retention of complex subjects. For example, students studying environmental science might engage in virtual field trips that allow them to explore ecosystems without leaving their classrooms. This hands-on approach can significantly boost engagement levels and foster deeper connections with the material.

Â The integration of **blockchain technology** is also expected to revolutionize credentialing processes within education. By providing secure and verifiable records of academic achievements, blockchain can streamline hiring practices for employers while empowering learners with ownership over their credentials. This shift towards decentralized record-keeping may lead to increased trust in qualifications and a reduction in fraudulent claims.

Â Finally, as remote work becomes increasingly normalized, the demand for **collaborative online tools** will continue to rise. Educational platforms that promote teamwork among students from diverse geographical backgrounds will prepare them for a globalized workforce. Enhanced features such as real-time collaboration on projects or peer-to-peer feedback mechanisms will further enrich the learning experience.

Â Together, these predictions highlight a future where educational technology not only enhances traditional methods but also redefines how knowledge is acquired and shared globally.

12.3 Preparing Students for a Tech-Driven Future

As we transition into an era dominated by technology, preparing students for a tech-driven future is paramount. This preparation goes beyond mere familiarity with devices; it encompasses a comprehensive understanding of digital literacy, critical thinking, and adaptability in an ever-evolving landscape. Educational institutions must prioritize equipping students with the skills necessary to thrive in this new environment.

 One crucial aspect of this preparation is fostering **digital literacy**. In today's world, being digitally literate means more than knowing how to use software or navigate the internet. It involves understanding how to critically evaluate information sources, protect personal data, and engage responsibly in online communities. Schools can implement curricula that emphasize these skills through project-based learning and real-world applications, ensuring that students are not just consumers of technology but also informed creators.

 Collaboration and communication skills are equally vital in a tech-driven future. As remote work becomes commonplace, students must learn to collaborate effectively across digital platforms. Educators can facilitate this by incorporating tools like video conferencing and collaborative document editing into classroom activities. By working on group projects that require virtual teamwork, students will develop essential interpersonal skills that are crucial for success in any career path.

 The integration of **problem-solving and critical thinking exercises** into the curriculum is another effective strategy for preparing students. Technology often presents complex challenges that require innovative solutions. By engaging students in coding challenges, robotics competitions, or design thinking workshops, educators can cultivate a mindset geared towards exploration and resilience—qualities that will serve them well in their future careers.

 Finally, fostering an **entrepreneurial spirit** among students can empower them to navigate the uncertainties of a tech-driven economy confidently. Programs that encourage creativity and innovation—such as hackathons or startup incubators—can inspire students to think outside the box and pursue their ideas passionately. This entrepreneurial mindset not only prepares them for potential self-employment but also equips them with the agility needed to adapt within traditional job markets.

Â Together, these strategies create a robust framework for preparing students for a tech-driven future where they can thrive as informed citizens and innovative professionals.

13

Psychological Aspects of AI-Assisted Learning

13.1 Understanding Student Motivation

Â Understanding student motivation is crucial in the context of AI-assisted learning, as it directly influences engagement, persistence, and overall academic success. In a landscape where artificial intelligence plays a pivotal role in education, recognizing what drives students to learn becomes even more essential. This section explores various motivational theories and their implications for integrating AI into educational practices.

Â One prominent theory is Self-Determination Theory (SDT), which posits that motivation is enhanced when individuals feel autonomous, competent, and connected to others. In an AI-assisted learning environment, personalized learning experiences can foster autonomy by allowing students to choose their learning paths and pace. For instance, an AI system could analyze a student's strengths and weaknesses, offering tailored resources that align with their interests while promoting mastery of subjects.

 Moreover, the role of intrinsic versus extrinsic motivation cannot be overlooked. Intrinsic motivation—driven by personal interest or enjoyment—can lead to deeper engagement with material. AI can support this by providing interactive content that resonates with students' passions or real-world applications of knowledge. Conversely, extrinsic motivators such as grades or rewards can also be effective but may not sustain long-term interest if overemphasized. Balancing these motivational factors is key in designing effective AI-driven educational experiences.

 Additionally, social interaction remains a significant component of student motivation. While AI can facilitate individualized learning experiences, it should not replace the human element entirely. Collaborative projects or peer interactions supported by AI tools can enhance social connections among students, fostering a sense of community that motivates them to engage more deeply with their studies.

In conclusion, understanding student motivation within the framework of AI-assisted learning involves recognizing the interplay between autonomy, competence, social connection, and both intrinsic and extrinsic factors. By leveraging these insights effectively, educators can create enriching environments where technology complements traditional teaching methods while keeping students motivated throughout their lifelong learning journeys.

13.2 Managing Anxiety Related to Technology Use

In the context of AI-assisted learning, managing anxiety related to technology use is a critical aspect that educators and institutions must address. As students increasingly rely on digital tools for their education, the potential for technology-induced anxiety can hinder their learning experiences and overall academic performance. Understanding the sources of this anxiety and implementing effective strategies to mitigate it is essential for fostering a positive learning environment.

Â One significant source of anxiety stems from the rapid pace of technological change. Many students may feel overwhelmed by the constant updates and new features in educational software, leading to feelings of inadequacy or fear of falling behind. To combat this, educators can provide structured training sessions that familiarize students with the tools they will be using. By creating a supportive atmosphere where questions are encouraged, students can build confidence in their ability to navigate these technologies.

Â Another contributing factor is the fear of making mistakes in a digital environment, which can be exacerbated by public sharing features often found in AI-assisted platforms. Students may worry about how their peers perceive them based on their online performance or contributions. To alleviate this concern, educators should emphasize a growth mindset, encouraging students to view mistakes as opportunities for learning rather than failures. Incorporating anonymous feedback mechanisms can also help reduce pressure during collaborative activities.

Â Moreover, balancing screen time is crucial in managing technology-related anxiety. Prolonged exposure to screens can lead to fatigue and increased stress levels among students. Educators should promote healthy habits by integrating breaks into lessons and encouraging offline activities that foster social interaction and physical movement. This holistic approach not only reduces anxiety but also enhances overall well-being.

Â Finally, fostering open communication about technology-related challenges is vital. Creating forums or support groups where students can share their experiences allows them to realize they are not alone in facing these issues. By addressing concerns collectively, institutions can develop tailored resources that specifically target common anxieties associated with technology use.

13.3 Building Resilience Through Independent Learning

Â Building resilience through independent learning is a crucial aspect of education, particularly in the context of AI-assisted learning environments. As students engage with technology, they are not only acquiring knowledge but also developing essential skills that foster resilience—an ability to adapt and thrive amidst challenges. This section explores how independent learning nurtures resilience and prepares students for future uncertainties.

 One of the primary benefits of independent learning is that it encourages self-directedness. When students take charge of their own educational journeys, they learn to set goals, manage their time effectively, and seek out resources independently. This autonomy cultivates a sense of ownership over their learning process, which can significantly enhance their confidence and motivation. For instance, a student who navigates an AI-driven platform to explore topics at their own pace may encounter obstacles but learns to overcome them without relying solely on external guidance.

 Moreover, independent learning fosters critical thinking and problem-solving skills. In an AI-assisted environment, learners often face complex tasks that require them to analyze information critically and devise solutions independently. This process not only builds cognitive skills but also instills a mindset geared towards perseverance. Students learn that setbacks are part of the learning journey; thus, they become more resilient in facing academic challenges as they develop strategies for overcoming difficulties.

Additionally, the integration of reflective practices into independent learning can further enhance resilience. Encouraging students to reflect on their experiences—what worked well and what didn't—allows them to internalize lessons learned from both successes and failures. Such reflection promotes adaptability as students recognize that each experience contributes to their growth. For example, after completing a challenging project using AI tools, a student might reflect on the strategies employed and adjust their approach for future tasks based on this insight.

Finally, fostering a supportive community around independent learners can amplify resilience-building efforts. Peer collaboration in online forums or study groups allows students to share experiences and strategies for overcoming challenges encountered during self-directed projects. This communal support reinforces the idea that resilience is not just an individual trait but can be cultivated collectively through shared experiences.

14

Policy Implications for Educational Reform

14.1 Governmental Roles in Transitioning Education

Â The role of government in transitioning education is pivotal, as it shapes the framework within which educational reforms can take place. As society evolves and technology advances, governments must adapt their policies to foster an environment conducive to innovative learning methods. This transition not only involves updating curricula but also rethinking the entire educational ecosystem to integrate artificial intelligence (AI) effectively.

Â One of the primary responsibilities of government is to establish a clear vision for education that aligns with future workforce needs. By collaborating with industry leaders and educational experts, policymakers can create a roadmap that emphasizes skills such as critical thinking, creativity, and digital literacy. For instance, countries like Singapore have successfully implemented national strategies that prioritize STEM education and lifelong learning, ensuring students are equipped for the demands of a rapidly changing job market.

 Furthermore, governments play a crucial role in funding and resource allocation. Transitioning to an AI-driven educational model requires significant investment in technology infrastructure and teacher training programs. Governments must ensure equitable access to these resources across diverse socio-economic backgrounds. Initiatives such as grants for underfunded schools or partnerships with tech companies can help bridge this gap, allowing all students to benefit from advanced learning tools.

 In addition to funding, regulatory frameworks need to be established that support innovation while maintaining quality standards in education. Governments should encourage pilot programs that test new teaching methodologies involving AI without compromising student outcomes. By creating flexible regulations that allow for experimentation within schools, governments can facilitate a culture of continuous improvement and adaptation.

Â Lastly, stakeholder engagement is essential for successful transitions in education. Governments must actively involve teachers, parents, and students in the reform process to ensure their perspectives are considered. This collaborative approach fosters buy-in from all parties involved and helps create a more inclusive educational environment where everyone feels invested in the changes being made.

14.2 Funding Models for Innovative Schools

Â The funding models for innovative schools are crucial in shaping the educational landscape, particularly as institutions strive to implement new teaching methodologies and technologies. As traditional funding mechanisms often fall short in supporting innovation, it is essential to explore alternative approaches that can provide the necessary resources for these forward-thinking educational environments.

One promising model is the **public-private partnership (PPP)**, which leverages both governmental support and private investment. This approach allows schools to access additional funds while sharing risks and responsibilities with private entities. For instance, a school might collaborate with a technology company to develop a specialized curriculum that incorporates cutting-edge tools, thereby enhancing student engagement and learning outcomes. Such partnerships not only provide financial backing but also foster innovation through shared expertise.

Another effective funding model is the **grant-based system**, where schools apply for competitive grants aimed at fostering innovation. These grants can come from various sources, including government agencies, philanthropic organizations, and educational foundations. Successful examples include initiatives like the U.S. Department of Education's Innovation Fund, which supports projects that aim to improve student achievement through innovative practices. By securing grant funding, schools can pilot new programs without the immediate pressure of long-term financial commitments.

 Crowdfunding has also emerged as a viable option for innovative schools seeking additional resources. Platforms such as DonorsChoose.org allow educators to present specific project needs directly to potential donors, creating a community-driven approach to funding education. This model empowers teachers and engages parents and local communities in supporting their schools' unique initiatives.

 Lastly, implementing a **weighted student funding model** can ensure that resources are allocated equitably based on individual student needs rather than solely on enrollment numbers. This approach recognizes that students from diverse backgrounds may require different levels of support, thus allowing innovative schools to tailor their programs effectively while addressing equity concerns.

 In conclusion, exploring diverse funding models is essential for fostering innovation within schools. By embracing public-private partnerships, grant systems, crowdfunding initiatives, and weighted student funding models, educational institutions can secure the necessary resources to thrive in an ever-evolving landscape.

14.3 Legal Considerations Surrounding AI Use

Â The integration of artificial intelligence (AI) in educational settings raises significant legal considerations that must be addressed to ensure compliance with existing laws and regulations. As schools increasingly adopt AI technologies for personalized learning, administrative efficiency, and data analysis, understanding the legal landscape becomes crucial for educators and policymakers alike.

Â One primary concern is **data privacy**. Educational institutions are required to comply with laws such as the Family Educational Rights and Privacy Act (FERPA) in the United States, which protects student information from unauthorized disclosure. The use of AI often involves collecting vast amounts of data on students' performance and behavior, necessitating stringent measures to safeguard this information. Schools must ensure that any AI tools they implement have robust data protection protocols in place to prevent breaches that could expose sensitive student data.

Â Another critical aspect is **intellectual property rights**. As educators utilize AI-generated content or software developed by third parties, questions arise regarding ownership and copyright. Institutions need clear agreements outlining who retains rights over materials produced using AI technologies. This clarity is essential not only for protecting intellectual property but also for fostering innovation within educational environments.

Â **Liability issues** also come into play when deploying AI systems in schools. If an AI tool provides inaccurate recommendations or assessments leading to adverse outcomes for students, determining liability can be complex. Schools must consider whether they or the technology providers bear responsibility for any negative consequences arising from the use of these systems.

Â Furthermore, there are implications related to **equity and access**. The deployment of AI should not exacerbate existing inequalities within education. Legal frameworks may need to evolve to address concerns about bias in algorithms that could disadvantage certain groups of students based on race, socioeconomic status, or disability. Ensuring equitable access to AI resources is paramount in promoting fairness across diverse student populations.

Â In conclusion, navigating the legal considerations surrounding AI use in education requires a proactive approach from policymakers and school administrators. By addressing issues related to data privacy, intellectual property rights, liability concerns, and equity, educational institutions can harness the potential of AI while safeguarding their students' rights and well-being.

15

Case Studies of Successful Implementations

15.1 Schools Pioneering AI Integration

Â The integration of artificial intelligence (AI) in educational settings marks a transformative shift in how knowledge is imparted and acquired. Schools that are at the forefront of this movement are not merely adopting technology; they are redefining the educational landscape to foster independent learning, personalized instruction, and continuous engagement. This section explores several pioneering institutions that exemplify successful AI integration, highlighting their innovative practices and the impact on student learning.

Â One notable example is the **International School of Amsterdam**, which has implemented an AI-driven platform that tailors learning experiences to individual student needs. By analyzing data on student performance and preferences, the system recommends resources and activities that align with each learner's unique pace and style. This approach not only enhances academic outcomes but also cultivates a sense of ownership over one's education.

Another inspiring case is found at **Montgomery County Public Schools** in Maryland, where AI tools assist teachers in identifying students who may require additional support. The district employs predictive analytics to monitor attendance patterns and academic performance, enabling educators to intervene proactively before issues escalate. This data-informed strategy fosters a supportive environment where every student can thrive.

The **Summit Learning Program**, adopted by various schools across the United States, exemplifies a blended learning model powered by AI. Students engage with personalized learning plans while teachers act as mentors rather than traditional instructors. The program emphasizes project-based learning, allowing students to explore subjects deeply while developing critical thinking skills essential for future success.

These examples illustrate how schools pioneering AI integration are reshaping education into a more dynamic and responsive system. By leveraging technology to enhance personalization and support, these institutions prepare students not just for exams but for lifelong learning in an ever-evolving world. As more schools adopt similar strategies, the potential for widespread educational reform becomes increasingly tangible.

15.2 Analyzing Outcomes and Best Practices

 Analyzing outcomes and best practices in the context of AI integration in education is crucial for understanding the effectiveness of these technologies. As schools increasingly adopt AI-driven tools, it becomes essential to evaluate their impact on student learning, engagement, and overall educational quality. This analysis not only highlights successful strategies but also identifies areas for improvement, ensuring that institutions can adapt and refine their approaches to maximize benefits.

 One significant outcome observed in schools utilizing AI is the enhancement of personalized learning experiences. For instance, data from the

International School of Amsterdam indicates that students using tailored learning platforms show improved academic performance compared to traditional methods. By analyzing individual progress and preferences, educators can create customized pathways that cater to diverse learning styles. This practice underscores the importance of leveraging data analytics to inform instructional decisions.

Â Moreover, proactive intervention strategies have emerged as a best practice among districts like Montgomery County Public Schools. Their use of predictive analytics allows teachers to identify at-risk students early on, facilitating timely support interventions. This approach not only helps in addressing academic challenges but also fosters a culture of care within the school community. The success of such initiatives demonstrates how data-driven decision-making can lead to more effective educational outcomes.

Â Another noteworthy aspect is the role of teacher training in maximizing AI's potential in classrooms. Successful implementations often involve comprehensive professional development programs that equip educators with the skills needed to integrate technology effectively into their teaching practices. For example, schools adopting the Summit Learning Program emphasize ongoing mentorship for teachers, enabling them to guide students through personalized projects while maintaining high engagement levels.

 In conclusion, analyzing outcomes related to AI integration reveals critical insights into effective educational practices. By focusing on personalized learning experiences, proactive interventions, and robust teacher training programs, schools can harness the full potential of AI technologies. These best practices not only enhance student achievement but also contribute to creating a more responsive and inclusive educational environment.

15.3 Scaling Successful Models Nationwide

 Scaling successful educational models nationwide is a critical endeavor that can significantly enhance the quality of education across diverse regions. This process involves not only replicating effective practices but also adapting them to fit various local contexts, ensuring that all students benefit from innovative approaches. The importance of this scaling lies in its potential to bridge educational disparities and foster equitable access to high-quality learning experiences.

 A key aspect of scaling successful models is the establishment of robust frameworks for collaboration among stakeholders, including educators, policymakers, and community organizations. For instance, initiatives like the **Teach for America** program have demonstrated how partnerships can mobilize resources and expertise to implement proven teaching strategies in underserved areas. By fostering a culture of shared responsibility and collective action, these collaborations can facilitate the widespread adoption of effective educational practices.

 Moreover, leveraging technology plays a pivotal role in scaling successful models. Digital platforms enable the dissemination of best practices through online training modules and resource-sharing networks. Programs such as **Khan Academy** exemplify this approach by providing free access to high-quality instructional materials that teachers can utilize regardless of their geographical location. This democratization of resources ensures that even schools with limited funding can implement evidence-based strategies effectively.

Another crucial factor in scaling is continuous evaluation and feedback mechanisms. Implementing systems for monitoring outcomes allows educators to assess the effectiveness of scaled models and make necessary adjustments based on real-time data. For example, districts employing **data analytics** tools can track student performance metrics across multiple schools, identifying trends that inform instructional improvements and resource allocation.

In conclusion, scaling successful educational models nationwide requires a multifaceted approach that emphasizes collaboration, technology integration, and ongoing evaluation. By focusing on these elements, stakeholders can create an inclusive educational landscape where innovative practices are accessible to all students, ultimately leading to improved academic outcomes across diverse communities.

16

Challenges to Implementation

16.1 Resistance from Stakeholders

Â The transition to an educational system guided by artificial intelligence (AI) presents numerous challenges, with resistance from stakeholders being one of the most significant. This resistance can stem from various groups, including educators, parents, students, and policymakers, each with their own concerns and motivations. Understanding these perspectives is crucial for successfully implementing AI-driven education reforms.

Â Educators often express apprehension regarding the role of AI in the classroom. Many fear that their expertise may be undervalued or rendered obsolete as AI systems take on more instructional responsibilities. This concern is compounded by a lack of familiarity with technology; teachers who are not well-versed in digital tools may resist adopting new methods that require them to integrate AI into their teaching practices. For instance, a study showed that teachers who received comprehensive training were more likely to embrace technology than those who did not.

Â Parents also play a pivotal role in this resistance. Concerns about data privacy and the potential for AI to misinterpret or mishandle sensitive information about their children can lead to skepticism about its implementation in schools. Additionally, some parents worry that reliance on AI could diminish the human element of education, which they believe is essential for social development and emotional learning. Engaging parents through transparent communication and involving them in decision-making processes can help alleviate these fears.

Â Students themselves may exhibit resistance due to unfamiliarity with self-directed learning models facilitated by AI. The shift from traditional teacher-led instruction to a more autonomous learning environment can be daunting for many learners accustomed to structured guidance. To address this challenge, educational institutions must provide adequate support systems that help students navigate this new landscape effectively.

Â Finally, policymakers face pressure from various interest groups when considering reforms involving AI in education. Balancing innovation with accountability requires careful deliberation and stakeholder engagement to ensure that all voices are heard and considered in the decision-making process. By fostering collaboration among all parties involvedâ€"educators, parents, students, and policymakersâ€"the path toward an AI-enhanced educational system can become less contentious and more productive.

16.2 Technical Challenges and Solutions

Â The integration of artificial intelligence (AI) into educational systems is fraught with technical challenges that can impede effective implementation. Addressing these challenges is crucial for harnessing the full potential of AI in enhancing learning experiences. This section explores key technical hurdles and proposes viable solutions to overcome them.

Â One significant challenge is the interoperability of various AI systems with existing educational technologies. Many schools utilize a patchwork of software tools, which can lead to data silos and inefficiencies when trying to implement an AI solution that requires seamless data exchange. To address this, developers should prioritize creating open APIs (Application Programming Interfaces) that allow different systems to communicate effectively. By fostering a collaborative ecosystem where tools can share data, educators can gain comprehensive insights into student performance and tailor interventions accordingly.

Â Another pressing issue is the quality and availability of data necessary for training AI algorithms. In many cases, educational institutions lack access to high-quality datasets that reflect diverse learning environments and student demographics. This limitation can result in biased or ineffective AI models. To mitigate this risk, partnerships between educational institutions and tech companies should be encouraged to facilitate data sharing while ensuring compliance with privacy regulations. Additionally, implementing robust data collection methods within classrooms can help generate valuable datasets that improve AI accuracy over time.

 Furthermore, there are concerns regarding the scalability of AI solutions across different educational contexts. A tool that works well in one school may not yield the same results in another due to variations in resources, infrastructure, or teaching methodologies. To enhance scalability, it is essential for developers to design adaptable AI systems capable of customizing their functionalities based on specific institutional needs. Pilot programs can also be instrumental; by testing solutions in varied settings before widespread deployment, stakeholders can gather feedback and make necessary adjustments.

 Lastly, ongoing maintenance and support for AI systems pose a challenge as technology evolves rapidly. Educational institutions often lack the technical expertise required for troubleshooting or upgrading these systems effectively. Establishing dedicated support teams or collaborating with external tech partners can provide schools with the necessary resources to ensure their AI tools remain functional and up-to-date.

16.3 Maintaining Quality Amid Rapid Change

Â The rapid evolution of educational technologies, particularly with the integration of artificial intelligence (AI), presents a dual challenge: the need for innovation and the imperative to maintain quality in educational outcomes. As institutions adopt new tools and methodologies at an unprecedented pace, ensuring that these changes do not compromise educational standards becomes paramount.

Â One critical aspect of maintaining quality is establishing robust evaluation frameworks that can assess the effectiveness of new technologies in real-time. Traditional assessment methods may not suffice in a landscape characterized by constant change. Therefore, developing dynamic metrics that account for both qualitative and quantitative data is essential. For instance, incorporating student feedback alongside performance analytics can provide a more holistic view of how AI tools impact learning experiences.

Moreover, professional development for educators plays a vital role in sustaining quality amid technological shifts. Teachers must be equipped not only with technical skills but also with pedagogical strategies that leverage AI effectively. Continuous training programs should focus on integrating technology into existing curricula while emphasizing critical thinking and creativity—skills that are increasingly important in a tech-driven world. Collaborative learning communities can further enhance this process by allowing educators to share best practices and resources.

Another significant factor is stakeholder engagement, which includes students, parents, and community members. Their input can guide the implementation process and ensure that new technologies align with the needs and values of those they serve. Regular forums or surveys can facilitate open communication channels where stakeholders express their concerns or suggestions regarding technological changes.

Finally, it is crucial to foster an adaptive culture within educational institutions that embraces change while prioritizing quality assurance mechanisms. This involves creating policies that encourage experimentation with new tools while simultaneously implementing safeguards to monitor their impact on student learning outcomes. By balancing innovation with accountability, schools can navigate the complexities of rapid change without sacrificing educational integrity.

17

The Role of Research in Evolving Education

17.1 Importance of Ongoing Research

Â The significance of ongoing research in education cannot be overstated, particularly as we transition towards a more technologically integrated learning environment. Continuous research serves as the backbone for developing innovative educational practices and tools that align with the evolving needs of students and educators alike. As artificial intelligence becomes increasingly prevalent in guiding student learning, it is essential to understand how these technologies can be effectively implemented and improved through rigorous investigation.

Â One critical aspect of ongoing research is its role in identifying best practices for integrating AI into educational settings. For instance, studies examining the effectiveness of AI-driven personalized learning platforms can provide insights into how these systems enhance student engagement and knowledge retention. By analyzing data from diverse classrooms, researchers can uncover patterns that inform educators about which strategies yield the best outcomes, thereby fostering an adaptive learning environment tailored to individual student needs.

Â Moreover, ongoing research contributes to understanding the broader implications of technology on educational equity. Investigating how different demographics interact with AI tools allows stakeholders to address potential disparities in access and effectiveness. For example, research may reveal that certain populations benefit more from specific types of AI interventions, prompting educators to adjust their approaches accordingly to ensure all students receive equitable support.

Â Additionally, continuous inquiry into teacher roles within this new paradigm is vital. As teachers transition from primary knowledge providers to facilitators who assist AI-driven learning processes, understanding their evolving responsibilities through research helps shape professional development programs. This ensures that educators are equipped with the necessary skills and knowledge to effectively collaborate with technology in enhancing student outcomes.

In conclusion, ongoing research is indispensable for navigating the complexities of modern education systems influenced by artificial intelligence. It not only informs practice but also drives innovation and equity within educational frameworks. By prioritizing research efforts, we can create a dynamic learning landscape where both students and teachers thrive amidst technological advancements.

17.2 Collaborating with Academic Institutions

Collaboration between educational organizations and academic institutions is pivotal in fostering a research-driven approach to evolving education. Such partnerships not only enhance the quality of educational practices but also bridge the gap between theoretical knowledge and practical application. By leveraging the expertise of researchers, educators can implement evidence-based strategies that significantly improve student outcomes.

One of the primary benefits of collaboration is access to cutting-edge research and resources. Academic institutions often possess extensive databases, libraries, and research facilities that can be invaluable for educators seeking to innovate their teaching methods. For instance, partnerships can facilitate joint research projects where educators and researchers work together to explore new pedagogical approaches or assess the effectiveness of existing programs. This synergy allows for a more comprehensive understanding of educational challenges and fosters solutions grounded in empirical evidence.

Moreover, collaborating with academic institutions provides opportunities for professional development through workshops, seminars, and training sessions led by experts in various fields. These initiatives equip educators with the latest knowledge on emerging trends such as artificial intelligence in education or inclusive teaching practices. As teachers gain insights from ongoing research, they are better prepared to adapt their instructional strategies to meet diverse student needs effectively.

Â Additionally, such collaborations can lead to innovative curriculum development that reflects current research findings. By integrating academic insights into classroom practices, educators can create curricula that are not only relevant but also engaging for students. For example, incorporating findings from cognitive science about how students learn best can inform lesson planning and assessment methods.

Â Finally, these partnerships play a crucial role in addressing educational equity issues by ensuring that all students benefit from high-quality instruction informed by rigorous research. Collaborative efforts can focus on identifying gaps in access or achievement among different demographic groups, leading to targeted interventions designed to support underrepresented populations.

Â In conclusion, collaborating with academic institutions enriches the educational landscape by fostering a culture of inquiry and continuous improvement. Through shared resources and expertise, both educators and researchers contribute to creating an adaptive learning environment that meets the evolving needs of students in a rapidly changing world.

17.3 Sharing Findings with Educators

 Sharing research findings with educators is a critical component in the evolution of educational practices. It serves as a bridge between academic inquiry and classroom application, ensuring that teachers are equipped with the latest insights to enhance their instructional methods. This process not only empowers educators but also fosters a culture of continuous improvement within educational institutions.

 One effective method for disseminating research findings is through professional development workshops and seminars. These events provide educators with direct access to researchers who can explain complex concepts in an accessible manner. For instance, when researchers present their findings on effective literacy strategies, they can demonstrate practical applications that teachers can implement immediately in their classrooms. Such interactions create opportunities for dialogue, allowing educators to ask questions and share their experiences, which enriches the learning experience for all participants.

Â Additionally, leveraging technology plays a significant role in sharing research findings widely. Online platforms such as webinars, podcasts, and educational blogs allow for asynchronous learning opportunities where educators can engage with content at their own pace. For example, a series of podcasts featuring interviews with leading education researchers can provide valuable insights into emerging trends and evidence-based practices without requiring teachers to attend live sessions. This flexibility ensures that even those with demanding schedules can benefit from ongoing professional development.

Â Moreover, creating collaborative networks among educators encourages the sharing of best practices informed by research. Professional learning communities (PLCs) enable teachers to come together regularly to discuss recent studies and how these findings can be integrated into their teaching strategies. By fostering an environment where educators feel comfortable sharing successes and challenges related to implementing new ideas, schools can cultivate a supportive atmosphere conducive to innovation.

Â In conclusion, effectively sharing research findings with educators is essential for transforming educational practices. By utilizing diverse methods such as workshops, technology-driven resources, and collaborative networks, we ensure that teachers remain informed about the latest developments in education research. This ongoing exchange not only enhances teaching effectiveness but ultimately leads to improved student outcomes across various learning environments.

18

Envisioning the Future of Education

18.1 Long-Term Goals for Educational Transformation

Â The long-term goals for educational transformation are pivotal in redefining the learning landscape to meet the demands of a rapidly evolving world. As we envision a future where education is not merely a phase of life but a continuous journey, it becomes essential to establish clear objectives that guide this transformation. These goals aim to create an adaptive, personalized, and inclusive educational environment that empowers learners to thrive in their personal and professional lives.

Â One primary goal is the integration of artificial intelligence (AI) as a core component of the educational experience. By leveraging AI technologies, we can facilitate personalized learning pathways tailored to individual student needs and preferences. This approach not only enhances engagement but also fosters self-directed learning, allowing students to take ownership of their educational journeys. For instance, AI-driven platforms can analyze student performance data in real-time, providing immediate feedback and resources that cater specifically to each learner's strengths and weaknesses.

Â Another significant objective is the reimagining of traditional classroom structures into more flexible and collaborative environments. The conventional school day often confines students within rigid schedules; however, future education should embrace year-round learning models that promote lifelong education. This shift encourages continuous skill development and adaptability, essential traits in an ever-changing job market. Schools could transform into community hubs where learners of all ages gather for workshops, seminars, and collaborative projects that extend beyond academic subjects.

- Fostering critical thinking and problem-solving skills through project-based learning.
- Encouraging interdisciplinary approaches that connect various fields of study.
- Promoting social-emotional learning to develop well-rounded individuals capable of navigating complex societal challenges.

Â Ultimately, these long-term goals aim not only at enhancing academic achievement but also at nurturing responsible global citizens equipped with the skills necessary for success in an interconnected world. By prioritizing innovation in teaching methods and embracing technology as an ally rather than a replacement for educators, we can create a transformative educational ecosystem that prepares learners for the future.

18.2 Inspiring a New Generation of Learners

Â Inspiring a new generation of learners is crucial for fostering an educational environment that not only imparts knowledge but also ignites passion and curiosity. As we transition into an era characterized by rapid technological advancements and global interconnectedness, it becomes imperative to cultivate a mindset among students that embraces innovation, creativity, and critical thinking. This section explores various strategies to inspire learners, ensuring they are equipped to navigate the complexities of the future.

 One effective approach is the integration of experiential learning opportunities that connect classroom concepts with real-world applications. By engaging students in hands-on projects, internships, or community service initiatives, educators can help them see the relevance of their studies beyond textbooks. For instance, programs that involve local businesses or environmental organizations allow students to apply their skills in meaningful ways while developing a sense of social responsibility.

 Moreover, mentorship plays a pivotal role in inspiring young minds. Establishing mentorship programs where experienced professionals guide students can provide invaluable insights into various career paths and life skills. These relationships foster confidence and motivation as mentors share their experiences and challenges faced along their journeys. Schools can facilitate these connections through networking events or partnerships with local industries.

 Additionally, incorporating technology into learning environments can significantly enhance student engagement. Utilizing interactive tools such as virtual reality (VR) or gamified learning platforms allows students to explore complex subjects in immersive ways. For example, VR simulations can transport learners to historical events or scientific phenomena, making abstract concepts tangible and exciting.

- Encouraging collaboration through group projects that promote teamwork and communication skills.
- Highlighting diverse perspectives by integrating multicultural education into curricula.
- Fostering resilience by teaching students how to embrace failure as part of the learning process.

 Ultimately, inspiring a new generation of learners requires a multifaceted approach that prioritizes engagement, mentorship, and innovative practices. By creating an educational landscape that values creativity and adaptability, we empower students not just to succeed academically but also to become proactive contributors to society.

18.3 Conclusion and Call to Action

Â As we stand on the brink of a transformative era in education, it is essential to recognize that the future of learning hinges not only on technological advancements but also on our collective commitment to fostering an inclusive and dynamic educational environment. The call to action is clear: educators, policymakers, parents, and communities must unite to create a holistic framework that prioritizes student engagement, creativity, and critical thinking.

Â To achieve this vision, we must advocate for educational reforms that embrace innovative teaching methodologies. This includes integrating project-based learning into curricula, which allows students to tackle real-world problems collaboratively. By doing so, we empower learners to develop essential skills such as problem-solving and teamwork while simultaneously nurturing their passion for knowledge. Schools should be encouraged to adopt flexible learning environments that accommodate diverse learning styles and promote active participation.

Moreover, it is imperative that we invest in professional development for educators. Teachers are at the forefront of inspiring the next generation; thus, equipping them with the tools and resources necessary for effective instruction is vital. Ongoing training in technology integration and pedagogical strategies will enable educators to adapt their teaching methods to meet the evolving needs of students.

Community involvement plays a crucial role in this educational renaissance. Partnerships between schools and local organizations can provide students with mentorship opportunities and access to resources that enhance their learning experiences. Engaging families in the educational process fosters a supportive network that reinforces the value of education within society.

Finally, we must cultivate a culture of resilience among students by encouraging them to view challenges as opportunities for growth rather than setbacks. This mindset shift can be facilitated through programs focused on social-emotional learning (SEL), which equip students with coping strategies and emotional intelligence skills necessary for navigating life's complexities.

The future of education is not merely about adapting to change; it is about leading it with intention and purpose. Together, let us commit ourselves to this cause—transforming our educational landscape into one where every learner thrives as an innovative thinker and responsible global citizen.

References:

- Kolb, D. A. (1984). Experiential Learning: Experience as the Source of Learning and Development.
- Schunk, D. H., & Zimmerman, B. J. (2008). Motivation and Self-Regulated Learning: Theory, Research, and Applications.
- How People Learn: Brain, Mind, Experience, and School by Bransford, J. D., Brown, A. L., & Cocking, R. R.
- Hattie, J. (2009). Visible Learning: A Synthesis of Over 800 Meta-Analyses Relating to Achievement. Routledge.
- Darling-Hammond, L., & Bransford, J. (2005). Preparing Teachers for a Changing World. Jossey-Bass.

- Wiggins, G., & McTighe, J. (2005). Understanding by Design. ASCD.

- Luckin, R., et al. (2016). Intelligence Unleashed: An Argument for AI in Education.

- OECD. (2021). The Future of Education and Skills: Education 2030.

- Dweck, C. S. (2006). Mindset: The new psychology of success. Random House.

- UNESCO. (2021). Artificial Intelligence in Education: Challenges and Opportunities.

- Kram, K. E. (1985). Mentoring at Work: Developmental Relationships in Organizational Life.

- National Institute of Mental Health. (2021). The Importance of Mental Health in Education.

- Fullan, M. (2016). The New Meaning of Educational Change. Teachers College Press.

- Johnson, L., Adams Becker, S., & Cummins, M. (2014). NMC Horizon Report: 2014 Higher Education Edition.

- Pearson, P.D., & Gallagher, M.C.(1983) "The Instruction of Reading Comprehension." Contemporary Educational Psychology

Education Revolution: A Year-Round Journey with AI Mentors presents a transformative vision for the educational landscape, advocating for a shift from traditional methods to a more dynamic, technology-driven approach. The book emphasizes the integration of artificial intelligence as a central component in guiding students toward independent learning, thereby addressing the limitations of the current educational system.

 The main topics explored include the role of AI mentors in facilitating personalized education, where each student can learn at their own pace and according to their unique interests. This model allows teachers to transition into supportive roles, focusing on enhancing the learning experience rather than delivering content directly. The concept of year-round schooling is also introduced, promoting lifelong learning and continuous skill development beyond conventional academic calendars.

 Key points highlight the importance of adaptability in education, encouraging students to take ownership of their learning journeys while leveraging AI tools for research and problem-solving. Notable insights suggest that this revolution not only prepares students for future job markets but also fosters critical thinking and creativity by allowing learners to explore subjects deeply and independently.

Â Overall, the book advocates for an educational paradigm shift that embraces technology as an ally in nurturing informed, self-sufficient learners equipped for lifelong success.

SUMMARY

Chapter 1: The Need for Educational Reform

1.1 Historical Context of Education

1.2 Limitations of the Current System

1.3 Vision for a New Learning Paradigm

Chapter 2: Understanding Artificial Intelligence in Education

2.1 Definition and Types of AI

2.2 Role of AI in Personalized Learning

2.3 Ethical Considerations in AI Implementation

Chapter 3: The Role of Teachers in an AI-Driven Classroom

3.1 Transitioning Teacher Roles

3.2 Collaboration Between Teachers and AI

3.3 Professional Development for Educators

Chapter 4: Designing the AI Learning Environment

4.1 Infrastructure Requirements

4.2 Integrating Technology into Classrooms

4.3 Creating Interactive Learning Spaces

Chapter 5: Curriculum Development for Lifelong Learning

5.1 Shifting from Traditional to Adaptive Curricula

5.2 Incorporating Real-World Skills and Knowledge

5.3 Continuous Curriculum Evaluation and Improvement

Chapter 6: Student-Centered Learning Approaches

6.1 Fostering Independence in Learners

6.2 Encouraging Critical Thinking and Problem Solving

6.3 Supporting Diverse Learning Styles

Chapter 7: Assessment and Evaluation in an AI Framework

7.1 Redefining Success Metrics

7.2 Formative vs Summative Assessments

7.3 Utilizing Data Analytics for Student Progress

Chapter 8: Year-Round Learning Models

8.1 Benefits of Continuous Education

8.2 Structuring Flexible Learning Schedules

8.3 Balancing Academic and Personal Growth

Chapter 9: Community Involvement and Support Systems

9.1 Engaging Parents and Guardians

9.2 Building Partnerships with Local Organizations

9.3 Creating Support Networks for Students

Chapter 10: Addressing Equity and Accessibility Issues

10.1 Ensuring Equal Access to Technology

10.2 Strategies for Inclusive Education

10.3 Overcoming Barriers to Participation

Chapter 11: Global Perspectives on AI in Education

11.1 Case Studies from Around the World

11.2 Lessons Learned from International Practices

11.3 Adapting Global Innovations Locally

Chapter 12: Future Trends in Educational Technology

12.1 Emerging Technologies Impacting Education

12.2 Predictions for the Next Decade

12.3 Preparing Students for a Tech-Driven Future

Chapter 13: Psychological Aspects of AI-Assisted Learning

13.1 Understanding Student Motivation

13.2 Managing Anxiety Related to Technology Use

13.3 Building Resilience Through Independent Learning

Chapter 14: Policy Implications for Educational Reform

14.1 Governmental Roles in Transitioning Education

14.2 Funding Models for Innovative Schools

14.3 Legal Considerations Surrounding AI Use

Chapter 15: Case Studies of Successful Implementations

15.1 Schools Pioneering AI Integration

15.2 Analyzing Outcomes and Best Practices

15.3 Scaling Successful Models Nationwide

Chapter 16: Challenges to Implementation

16.1 Resistance from Stakeholders

16.2 Technical Challenges and Solutions

16.3 Maintaining Quality Amid Rapid Change

Chapter 17: The Role of Research in Evolving Education

17.1 Importance of Ongoing Research

17.2 Collaborating with Academic Institutions

17.3 Sharing Findings with Educators

Chapter 18: Envisioning the Future of Education

18.1 Long-Term Goals for Educational Transformation

18.2 Inspiring a New Generation of Learners

18.3 Conclusion and Call to Action

www.ingramcontent.com/pod-product-compliance
Lightning Source LLC
Chambersburg PA
CBHW052207220526
45471CB00004B/1852